Voices
From
The Wall

Compiled by Jan C. Scruggs
FOUNDER AND PRESIDENT
Vietnam Veterans Memorial Fund

For more information:

Vietnam Veterans Memorial Fund
1012 14th Street, NW, Suite 201
Washington, DC 20005-3406
202-393-0090 phone, 202-393-0029 fax
www.vvmf.org, email us at vvmf@vvmf.org

In Memory of
Libby Hatch
1955–1998

Libby Hatch
Director of Special Projects for the
Vietnam Veterans Memorial Fund

Elizabeth Denison Hatch was known simply as Libby to her family, countless friends and Vietnam veterans across the country. She worked for the Vietnam Veterans Memorial Fund for seven years. She moved quickly in life, just as quickly as she left our lives. She loved those warm, sunny days when she could take her motorcycle for a ride and leave the confines of the city. She died in a motorcycle accident on December 6, 1998.

Throughout her too-short life Libby touched the hearts and souls of everyone she met—whether she was placing a pin on a veteran's lapel, handing a bouquet of flowers to an elderly woman walking down the street or giving a twenty-dollar bill to a homeless man. Libby perfected the art of the small gesture. She always knew how to lift someone's spirits with her overtures of comfort and friendship. She often carried a dark marking pen with her which she used to remove Nazi Swastikas placed in public places by vandals in Washington, DC.

From the start of her life in Greenwich, CT, Libby was always marching to her own tune. She finished high school in three years, went on to attend St. John's College in Annapolis and was graduated from Emerson College where she received a B.S. in Mass Communications. Libby moved to the Washington, DC area in 1976. In 1991, Libby became a staff member of the Vietnam Veterans Memorial Fund. She worked tirelessly to organize many events at the Wall, including the annual Memorial Day and Veterans Day ceremonies.

Libby's spirit lives on in the hearts of all who were blessed enough to have known her.

Thank you, Libby for being a True Friend to us all.

TABLE OF CONTENTS

Page

Foreword
By Jan Scruggs

Since the dedication in 1982, the Wall has done much to heal the nation's wounds after the bitterly divisive experience of the Vietnam War. For those who served, that year marked a sea change in the country's view of the Vietnam veteran. Americans began to understand and respect the Vietnam veterans' service and sacrifice.

Yet just as the Memorial helped heal wounds of veterans, so too did its creation help to heal the nation. Supporters and opponents of the Vietnam War cooperated to bring about the magnificent chevron-shaped Memorial. Many tears have been shed and millions of people have had their emotions touched by the two granite walls filled with names.

Medal of Honor Recipient Brian Thacker recently said of the Vietnam Veterans Memorial, "What started as a symbol of healing has become a vehicle for education." *Voices From The Wall* is a book that was written to remind people of the healing that is still needed and further, to help educate young and old about the ongoing legacy of the Vietnam War.

In *Voices,* we have gathered authors, journalists, educators and veterans to share their stories about the Vietnam War and the Wall's impact. Each author brings a unique perspective and a longing to tell their story. Some continue to argue about Vietnam. Historians will forever debate that conflict. Yet no one can dispute the many ways that Vietnam touched people's lives: here are some of their stories.

I would like to thank all of our authors for helping to create this book. The beauty of the Memorial is that it lends itself to so many different emotions, interpretations, and experiences. This is well illustrated in the melange of writings in the following pages.

I want also to thank *Michelle Hopkins* and *Jesse Ferguson* for their invaluable service as proofreaders (the mantle of a proofreader is a heavy one—he or she gets all the blame for the overlooked typographical error but no one sees the glory of the caught mistake); *Maurice Chaite, Katherine Griffin,* and *Holly Rotondi* for their able assistance; *George Mayo* for his wisdom and guidance; and *Libby Hatch* for her editing, design, and cover photo. I would like to thank *Maya Lin,* without whom this unique, imaginative, and personal Wall of stone built into the sheltering arms of earth would never have been conceived.

Lastly, I would like to thank you, dear reader, and hope that you will share this book with others that might be interested in the Vietnam Veterans Memorial.

A Visit
By Norma Golub

Norma Golub of Brooklyn, NY wrote this poem after visiting the Memorial in 1993, in memory of her brother, Howard H. Rabinowitz, who died in the invasion of Normandy.

'Twas black that night in D.C.
A dense heavy blackness covering me,
Covering our guide with his
Dark open umbrella for us to follow.

The foot path to the Monument
Could be felt more easily than seen.
I approached in awe as
The monument started a few inches high.

Gradually growing in immensity of horror,
Disbelief and forever, I was aware of
Thousands of names engraved and
I ran my fingers lightly
What was trapped within this wall.

Try to transfer feelings by feel,
Mentally my fingers re-arranged letters
And I FOUND MY BROTHER, who died in St. Lo,
France, World War II 1944.

My fingers tingled with searing buried memories,
I found my brother
I can cry for all.

The Lessons of War
By Senator Chuck Hagel (R-NE)

Senator Hagel and his brother, Tom, served together in Vietnam. Their combat experiences were chronicled in war correspondent Myra McPherson's Long Time Passing.

For many Americans, the Vietnam War was the determining factor of their lives. For the over 58,000 men and women whose names are inscribed on the black granite panels of the Vietnam Veterans Memorial, the war in Vietnam marked the end of their lives. My brother, Tom, and I have many friends and comrades whose names are on those panels. People we will never forget. They are people our nation must never forget either.

After the Vietnam War ended, our country tried to forget Vietnam as quickly as possible. It was an unusual, and hopefully isolated, occurrence in our nation's history.

As American soldiers, sailors, airmen and Marines returned home, they faced a situation never before endured by our troops: open hostility from many neighbors and former classmates. They left as teenagers and they returned as men and women. Most quickly put away their uniforms and tried to integrate into civilian life as quietly as possible. For those who fought the war and those who protested it, the less said about Vietnam, the better.

During the '70s, Vietnam was simply never mentioned in casual conversation. It was as though it never happened. The war developed into an ugly wound, festering just beneath polite society, ready to erupt at any time when people of differing opinions about

Vietnam gathered in the same room.

For those veterans who returned home, it was a time of bitter emptiness. It was a solitary time when the nightmarish thoughts of combat and memories of friends lost could not be understood by those who remained behind. Those who fought in Vietnam wanted to forget the heat, the fear, and mostly, the blood. Those who opposed the war wanted to forget the insanity of sending young men to die in a war the government was not committed to winning. Neither side was totally successful.

When Jan Scruggs conceived the idea of a memorial to those who fought in Vietnam, he wanted to make it impossible for *anybody* to ever forget. And, hopefully, impossible for our leaders to ever make the same mistakes again.

That's the reason that the Vietnam War still matters. If this war taught us anything, it is that our nation must make a total commitment to victory whenever we commit our fighting men and women. If we're not willing to make this commitment, then we must keep those troops at home.

The Vietnam Veterans Memorial has allowed those who opposed the war to honor the warrior without honoring the war. It has allowed those of us fortunate enough to return to pay our respects to our fallen comrades. It has truly become The Wall That Heals for millions of Americans.

Most importantly, the Memorial is a beautiful and haunting instructor. The Memorial teaches our children and future generations that war is neither glamorous nor glorified. Men and women die in war, and usually these men and women are very young. At the very least, those who die should not have to die in vain. We owe it to them and we owe it to our children to make sure this does not happen.

The lessons of war must be passed on to our children and taught in our schools.

[The Wall] did a great job showing me what war is really all about ... I had to cover my face so no one would see my tears for all those that died in the war.

Evan, age 16

Time To Put Divisions Aside
By Terry Anderson

Terry Anderson was a Marine in Vietnam. While a reporter for Associated Press, he was captured and held hostage for seven years in Lebanon by Hezbollah guerrillas. He gave this speech at the Wall in 1992.

Is everybody cold and wet? Does that bring back memories? I can't tell you what it has felt like today [at the Vietnam Veterans Memorial 10th Anniversary Veterans Day Ceremony, 1992] to have people come up and shake my hand and say welcome home. It's a double homecoming for me. I don't think I have to tell you because I think most of you know. You know the feeling very well.

Did you know that somebody left a Congressional Medal of Honor this morning at the Wall? There's no name on it and nobody was able to tell me who it belonged to or who left it, but it's the second one that's been left here. I don't know what the people who left those medals were trying to say with their action. I know what it says to me. It says that this is a fitting place for the nation's highest honor and that honor should be shared by everybody listed on that Wall.

A couple of days ago, I received a copy of a letter to the editor of the Poughkeepsie, New York Journal, written by a gentleman who is objecting to me speaking here today. He was apparently unaware that I served six years in the U.S. Marine Corps, including a tour in Vietnam. He went on to say that only veterans should speak at the Wall, not political hostages. It was sent to me by another

Marine. Now I don't object to this man not knowing I'm a former Marine—although I'm very proud of that fact—but I couldn't disagree more with his main point.

This memorial is dedicated to those who gave their lives in Vietnam. It is a most fitting memorial and a beautiful one. It is one that promotes, even demands, our homage to these men and women. But it seems to me that it is also a penetrating reminder that they were not the only ones who paid a price in that war, great as theirs was. Veteran or civilian, supporter or opponent of that terrible war, we all paid. We all have the right to speak our thoughts here, to remember aloud what it cost us individually and as a nation. President Bush once said that it was time to put an end to the divisions the Vietnam War engendered in America. Now we know presidents don't really expect to be taken seriously when they make such statements and sometimes they don't even take themselves seriously. But this is one I think we should take very seriously, indeed.

It was a time of great passion, deep anger, and deep commitment to ideas that were worthy of such intensity. It taught us much about ourselves, about America, about the world. I don't suggest we forget those lessons; we can't and we shouldn't, just as we can never forget the courage and the sacrifice of the people whose names are written here. But the divisions, yes, it's time we put those behind us, time we acknowledged that both those who served and those who refused, those who fought for America and those who fought against her, did so because they all believed passionately that what they were doing was right.

We have a bright, new chance to move forward in

America, to achieve great things, to solve great problems. We can only do so in cooperation. We have the same chance in the world and we face the same demand, that of cooperation. Not division, not recrimination, not holding onto old enmities and bitterness. The quiet grandeur and the nobility of this beautiful memorial demands of us an equal nobility. It demands forgiveness and reconciliation. I pray that we can live up to that demand.

I never really thought of Vietnam as any different from any other war. I actually couldn't even see the effects of any war until now. When we learn about war, we hear 1,000's killed and the more that die, the more severe the war. Thank you for letting me see what <u>really</u> happens.
Jillian, age 15

Sacrificed, But Not In Vain
By Rocky Bleier

Rocky Bleier was wounded in Vietnam and was told he could never play professional athletics. Through hard work and determination, he recovered and went on to play in two Superbowls with the Pittsburgh Steelers. This is from a speech he gave at the Wall.

For me, there's really no better place to be on Veterans Day than standing here at the Wall. Who better to share this experience with than all veterans from all wars? For that one single experience has bound us—including those names etched on this granite—together for all eternity because we have shared so much. Whether in a different time or place, the essence of war remains the same.

For the Vietnam veterans, in serving our country those many years ago, we came from across this nation and we were dispersed in I, II, III and IV Corps from the DMZ to the Delta, from Cambodia and Thailand to the coastal shore. We wore the patches of the Americal, the 25th, the 82nd, the 173rd, for the Fourth Marines, Big Red One, 101st to the 196th, representing the Army, Navy, Air Force, Coast Guard, and Marines. And we were privates, non-coms, and officers. We walked point, got ripped up by the elephant grass, our buddies watched our backs as we watched theirs.

And we fought with the big guns and the mortars, the M-79s, support and fighters, gunships and C-130s, we patrolled not only the rivers and the Mekong, but also the streets of Saigon all the way to Danang. We were the MPs, the infantry, and the intelligence. We were in finance, communications, personnel; we tended to the wounded and cared for those who had died. In that era, we were three, four, five million strong—we laughed, we cried, boy, we were afraid. We lost family, friends and loved ones and we were bored waiting for care packages and wrote love letters home. We looked forward to R&R rotation and becoming civilians once again.

We left one battlefield only to face another. We fought for dignity and we went back to making a living. And we will never, let me tell you, <u>never</u> forget them, those good people who we honor here today.

Somebody once said bad things happen when good people do nothing. Bad policies happen, like in Vietnam, when good people don't get involved. Bad people are elected when good people don't run for office. I would like you to consider the flip side of that premise: Good things happen when good people are willing to do what's right and good things happen when good people are willing to lay aside what is popular and profitable at the moment. Good things happen when good people are willing to overcome obstacles to do what they know is best.

This monument only stands because good people were willing to overcome those obstacles and get it built. Reflection and remembrance is a time for healing because it is right. Those names forever remembered here are of good people who were willing to do what they thought was right. This nation was founded by people like that. Some mighty good people pledged their lives, their futures and their sacred honor to do what they knew was right. And down through the years, our freedoms have been preserved by people like you and me and those who we honor, who have been willing to have those same beliefs.

I submit to you that ours will remain the land of the free only so long as it remains the home of brave, good people who are willing to stand up and be counted and do what they believe is right. Let this day and these monuments be reminders for future generations that the efforts and lives of some mighty good people have not been wasted in vain.

We never know the effects of war unless we experience it, but this Memorial shows how serious war really is.

Diane

A Decision Writ In Granite
By Q.X. Pham

On April 24, 1975, Q.X. Pham was evacuated from Saigon at the age of 10. He grew up in Oxnard, CA, and graduated from UCLA with a bachelor's degree. He served seven years on active duty as a U.S. Marine Corps helicopter pilot and flew combat and support missions during Operation Desert Storm and in Somalia. A major in the Marine Reserves, he now works in sales and lives in California. A frequent speaker about the Vietnam War and its effects on society, he is completing a book based upon his experiences. To read some of his previously published articles, please visit http://www.qxpham.com.

"Those who expect to reap the blessings of liberty must, like men, undergo the fatigues of supporting it."

—Thomas Paine

My decision to serve in the U.S. Marine Corps solidified the day I stood before the Wall. It was during the summer of 1986 and I was on liberty from Officer Candidates School (OCS) from nearby Quantico, VA. It had been a long, hot, tortuous and physically demanding summer. But the emotional toll of being one of the first Vietnamese-Americans to undertake the OCS was the greatest. I knew the reputation of South Vietnamese as poor soldiers remained on the minds of some OCS staff, especially the Vietnam veterans. Yet I also had a father who suffered in re-education camp because he remained and fought until the day Saigon fell. I wanted to uphold his honor more than anything.

The officer's commission and the accompanied honors

faded from my mind after the first week at OCS. I merely wanted to graduate. The often used word at OCS—"Unsat" (meaning unsatisfactory)—haunted me every time I felt I could no longer keep up on a forced march or a long run through the woods. Throughout the summer as I watched training films and recalled Hollywood movies, images of Marines killing Asians on the battlefields of the South Pacific, Korea, and Vietnam left an indelible mark on me. I felt Asians had been demonized as a result of the Corps' illustrious combat history. I had temporarily concluded the Marine Corps way of life and mission incompatible with my reason to serve.

My classmate, Mark Henderson, whose father was a Vietnam veteran, suggested that we visit the Wall during our last liberty weekend prior to graduation. It was difficult to stand before those who gave up their lives to fight for my own freedom. Yet I didn't even recognize one name. They were not even from my country—how could they have sacrificed their lives for my countrymen and me across the globe and 12,000 miles away? Why didn't they go to Canada? Why didn't they question their orders? Where would I be now if they didn't intervene and fight the Communists? What would their lives be like now had they lived? Up until that point, my main goal was just to complete OCS and return to civilian life. At the Wall, I realized the sacrifice of those whose names were inscribed was the reason I was standing there that day. I accepted my commission a year later.

The night I left Saigon, I thought I'd never see war again. On a dark and humid spring morning, my family was rushed onto a U.S. aircraft headed for freedom. A life of youth and happiness amid a war in our backyard came to an end. Had my family remained in Vietnam, I was destined to become a soldier. I would have followed in my father's footsteps to become a pilot in the Vietnamese Air Force had the war continued. Or I could have been shipped out to fight the Khmer Rouge in Cambodia had we not gotten out of Vietnam in April of 1975. Instead of wearing the uniform for the Army of the Republic of Vietnam, I realized my dreams of soldiering in America. The day the Gulf War ended, I felt I had earned my American citizenship and paid back my debt to our great nation. I would have never felt that way had I not paid homage to those who spoke out to me at the Wall.

The only name I recognized on the Wall during my second visit was that of Terrence C. Graves, Second Lieutenant, USMC, KIA 1968, and recipient of the Medal of Honor. He was 22. A portrait of Lieutenant Graves hung on the first floor of Graves Hall, a bachelor officers' quarters used to house newly commissioned officers undergoing the Basic School. In the painting, he wore his dress blues without any decorations and appeared like the rest of the young lieutenants running around Graves Hall 20 years later. I used to stare at his portrait during my six-month stay at Graves Hall and wonder if I could ever live up to his sacrifice and those of others on the Wall.

More than 30 years after the first American combat troops landed in Vietnam, the blame continues. Some Vietnam veterans say the press lost the war. The South Vietnamese blame the Americans for abandoning them on the battlefield. The protesters claim their efforts saved lives. The generals condemn their civilian leadership.

The veterans angrily reject our current President. The South Vietnamese who live under the Communist regime wonder if their leaders tried hard enough. The question of responsibility rages on decades later.

I recall something I read about warmongers prior to going to Saudi Arabia in 1990. A warmonger is a person who is invincible in peace and invisible in war. A warmonger is a man who is always ready to lay down your life for his country. Those whose names were inscribed on the Wall laid down their lives for me and my former country. They were not warmongers. I sincerely hope I have honored their sacrifice with my own service. For the students, just know that the dead served. The dead did not point the finger at anyone. The dead are blameless. They must be remembered and honored.

While I was in Vietnam in 1970, I ran across a saying. I don't know who the author was, but it has left a lasting impression on me.
  For those who fought for it
  Freedom is the taste the
  Protected will never know.
In a very few words, it says a lot.

The Soldier's Dilemma
By Thomas E. Bulleit, Jr.

Tom Bulleit saw combat with the Marines in Vietnam. He is an attorney and President of the Bulleit Distilling Co. in Kentucky.

This land and its immigrants have evolved into a nation, a people, the Rainbow Tribe. Our hopes and dreams are fact and law. We have freedoms unknown in human history. We have those whose names are upon this Wall to thank for this democracy and its maintenance. Those whose names are upon this Wall and those whose names could have been upon this Wall, those sons and daughters, mothers and fathers are of the human tribe. And as such, their experience often had a confusing duality.

I believe the soldier's experience not to be unique, so I will relate my experience as one shared. My father was a soldier. He served in the Third Army Tank Corps in the Second World War. He lost his right eye in the Battle of the Bulge. I had a real hero and grew up playing soldier. When my turn came, I was proud to serve with the Marine Corps. My father's only advice was to write mother often and each time assure her that I was safe and far from action, no matter what the actual circumstances may be.

I have never been so aware of passing from and to. Though sad, my father was proud of me. I had accomplished a son's primary goal and redeemed a poor college performance. When I left for Vietnam, I could see in my mother's eyes as she said goodbye that it is easier to go than to wait. My father saw this, too, maybe for the first time. He was young, and dashing, and naïve when he went to war. For me, there was pain in leaving and thrill in going.

In the aftermath of first combat, seeing the dead, the wounded, I thought but did not say, what can bring men to this? And then, in a service for the dead, feeling lost and abandoned, our spirits were lifted to pride as a Marine sang a cappella that call to glory, "The Battle Hymn of the Republic." "The Battle Hymn of the Republic" was also sung at my father's funeral. Our service became a strong, though unspoken, bond between us.

When I returned home, "back to world" we said, to a proud father and mother who had aged more than time would merit, I began law school on the G.I. Bill. One evening, while watching a documentary on the Rolling Thunder bombing campaign, again the question arose, "What have we done? How could it have come to this?"

Pride and shame would not seem to be bedfellows, but they were for me. I began to understand my father's quiet acceptance of a soldier's dilemma. In defending our humanity, our human rights, and our democracy, sometimes we must be inhumane, sometimes we must kill and sometimes we must be killed. Pride and bitterness would not seem to be bedfellows, but they were for me. I carried the bitterness that I served without appreciation when others hadn't served at all, the bitterness that my father had sacrificed so much with little appreciation.

Many years after returning home, I sat on the patio with my father and was struck by the thought that he was not bitter—he was joyful. He was joyful and thankful to have survived. My bitterness turned to shame, which turned to gratitude. My old soldier had given his good advice, a lesson he could not have taught with words.

The duality of experience was not unique to those we honor here today, but was rather experienced on a national basis. I was in Vietnam during the political campaigns of 1968, but witnessing their dramatization in the film "Born on the Fourth of July" was a heartbreaking experience. Witnessing our nation, our people holding strong beliefs so desperate was reminiscent of my home state, Kentucky, and the role it played during the Civil War. During the Vietnam War, a Marine general has been quoted as responding to what he thought of war protesters and flag-burning as follows: "The lives of my Marines dying in the field will have been wasted if our democratic rights are not preserved."

In this duality of experience, courage and fear, honor and guilt, there is confusion, but these emotions so juxtaposed are what make us the human tribe. My old soldier is gone and I have taken his place. May I be worthy of it.

For those whose names could have been upon this Wall, let us be as good in action as we are in intention. For those whose names are upon this Wall, let us pray:

Lord, make me an instrument of your peace. Where there is hatred, let me sow love. Where there is injury, let me sow pardon. Where there is doubt, let me sow faith. Where there is despair, let me give hope. Where there is darkness, let me give light. Where there is sadness, let me give joy. Oh, Lord, grant that I may not try to be comforted, but to comfort; not try to be understood, but to understand; not try to be loved, but to love, because it is in giving that we receive. It is in forgiving that we are forgiven and it is in dying that we are born to eternal life.

*You were very brave to go and fight for our country.
My dad was in the army, but he didn't have to fight in a
war. Thank you for keeping our country free. All veterans
are heroes. I love all of you.*

Billy, age 7

Vietnam In America's Memory
By Robert O. Muller

Robert Muller is the president of the Vietnam Veterans of America Foundation.

I have never been satisfied with my efforts to describe what it felt like to take a bullet the way I did in April of 1969. Since the pain was beyond pain it didn't really hurt. It was as if I smashed my thumb with a hammer. In those first moments you are not aware you really did a number on yourself. Your only sense is of numbed tingling—but you know it's about to get very serious.

When the bullet went through my chest it punched holes in both my lungs and severed the spinal chord. The immediate sensation was feeling like a windshield on a car that had just shattered into a thousand pieces. Another way to describe it is as if I were in some gigantic gong that got slammed with a really big sledgehammer. Seconds later there was nothing left but total stillness and complete concentration on my immediate life force which was starting to fade out. I was aware that I was starting to recede from consciousness and that I was dying. A comforting calmness and warmth seemed to surround me as I felt life slip away. I cannot adequately convey how certain I was that I was going to die right then and there. I was overwhelmed. There was nothing I could do to stop what was happening—nothing more that I could say to anyone—nothing I could hold onto or take. It was time to go.

I awoke on the hospital ship USS Repose. I was in intensive care with tubes sticking in and out of my body and lots of things going on around me. I would later learn that despite an almost immediate helicopter medevac (and the fortunate placement of the hospital ship right off the coast) entered into my records was the note that had I arrived one minute later I would have surely died. It turned out that both lungs had collapsed and my body was shutting down. The experience of dying was very real.

From the moment I regained consciousness, my reaction to being alive was disbelief and joy. I guess you really have to believe you are dying to appreciate what it means to be able to live. Since the injury left me a paraplegic, paralyzed from the chest down, many people tended to look at me in terms of loss. I've always looked at my life since that day as a gift, that I was really somehow granted a second chance at life. I have heard a lot of others say similar things, but I don't generally believe they mean it the same way I do. I live my life with an extraordinary awareness of being. I am very aware that life is finite.

The war also taught me some lessons in loss and suffering. The pain and agony was not confined to the battlefield. It continued in the hospitals that I stayed in for over a year, and in the years of helping other veterans and their families pick up the pieces of shattered lives. While appreciative of life, with so much suffering by so many, with so much despair and sorrow, it was necessary to answer the most basic question of all—why go on with a process that involves so much loss?

The answer for me was in what I was getting back from my fellow man in return for what I was giving out in efforts and concern for others. Love. Many were able to return from Vietnam and walk away from it all. Or at least make the attempt. I couldn't. I was left to share and better understand some of the costs of war and the need for assistance to put your life together. I learned to live for today and the future and let go of the past. I learned that the reward in life is in helping other people. I've been able to use my war experience, my disability, my rehabilitation and my reconciliation with my former adversaries as lessons to inform and credential my work with veterans, war victims, and other concerns around armed conflict. It's an experience I wouldn't trade for anything.

The Barrier You Have To Cross
By Roger D. Berry

Roger D. Berry served with the U.S. Air Force in Vietnam between 1965 and 1968, stationed at various times at Danang, Pleiku, Cam Ranh Bay and Tan Son Nhut.

After leaving Vietnam 30 years ago, I finally made it to the Wall this past Memorial Day 1998. The first few years I tried to forget, the last few years I couldn't forget, but while I couldn't get to the Wall for different reasons, I knew it was something I had to try.

I spent Saturday, Sunday and Monday at the Wall. I didn't know anybody, yet I knew everybody. I could tell the Vietnam veterans from the others. It is that look when you make eye contact. I was on this emotional roller coaster all weekend and I finally broke through that barrier you have to cross to move forward.

The drive home Memorial Day evening was very sad for me. Saying goodbye is never easy. It took so long to get there, I didn't want to leave.

I have met so many veterans who haven't been able to bring themselves to the Wall yet and the trip home was no exception. I was refueling in Harrisonburg, VA when a young lady approached me and said, "My dad has a hat like yours." I told her I had just been to the Wall after a long journey getting there. She said that she wanted to take her dad to the Wall, but every time she asked him they would just cry. I told her to be patient and then *we* just stood there and cried. Total strangers with a common bond.

After that, I crossed the street where upon a stranger

stopped me, who was a Vietnam veteran. We talked about
'Nam for a few minutes. Then he, too, wanted to know
if I had been to the Wall because he had driven from
Harrisonburg to D.C. and made it as far as the Lincoln
Memorial, at which point he turned around and went
home. He could not make it those last 300 yards. I told
him I knew how he felt, but to please keep trying.

While a lot of us were going backwards after the war,
Jan Scruggs and the Memorial Fund were going forward,
particularly at a time when it wasn't the most popular
thing to do. You and your team are real heroes for what
you have accomplished. There aren't enough handshakes,
hugs, or tears to express my feelings so I'll just say,
"Thanks, brother. Welcome home."

A Father's Day Rose
By Libby Hatch

Libby Hatch was the Director of Special Projects for the Vietnam Veterans Memorial Fund.

The Vietnam Veterans Memorial Fund has a number of programs that enable people who can't visit the Wall in person to participate in honoring our veterans. One of the more colorful ones takes place early on Father's Day.

At 6:30 a.m., across Constitution Avenue from the Wall, 50 volunteers converged and began attaching thousands of notes and letters to the long stemmed roses we had picked up from the hotel refrigerator earlier that morning, keeping them fresh and alive over the weekend. We attached one or more notes to one thousand red and yellow roses, the red representing those killed and the yellow representing those still missing.

Before the sun became too hot and the Wall too crowded, we crossed the street, everyone's arms brimming with color, and proceeded to make a large circle. One by one, every volunteer read a representative note aloud. The outpouring of emotions from all around the country—from fathers to their sons, from widows to their husbands, from children to the fathers they barely had time to know—was as wrenching as it was beautiful.

After everyone had a chance to share a reading, we made our way to whichever panel the loved one's name was located. Finding the name, we read aloud the note, touching the rose to the name before leaving it standing at the bottom of the panel.

Seeing the red and yellow bouquet cradled by the black

arms of the Wall and listening to the sound of hushed voices echoing from around the country was worth getting up that early to experience. If anyone is in Washington, DC on Father's Day, we welcome you to join us in the coming years.

This is one of the letters that were read this past Father's Day at the Wall:

In Remembrance of My Dad
By Jennifer Branch Denard

Jennifer Denard is the daughter of Captain William A. Branch, whose name can be found on Panel 9 West, Line 18. He died June 6, 1970.

Each year, I dream of what I would buy you for Father's Day, Dad. I scour the racks for the perfect card or present, and I buy it in my mind. I wish we could be together today. Just once. I would sit here with you at this Wall and listen and hug and love you.

I don't remember you. I was too young when you died. But in my heart, I know you Dad. I have read your letters and talked to your friends. I have learned more from you, despite your death, than I have in a lifetime of schooling. Your lessons to me are evident. They are gifts to me, Dad, that I treasure.

Thank you for loving Mom so much—for writing to her every day from that war. Lessons on how a man should treat a woman. Thank you for making me feel loved—for taking time to write me a letter before you died that day. Thank you for teaching me about conviction and bravery—for volunteering twice to go and fight for what is right. You were the first in your family to graduate from college. You wanted to make the world safer. You wanted to end communism. I am proud of you, Dad. I appreciate you. And I try hard to be like you. This is my gift to you. I love you.

   Little Miss Jen

Regarding Sean
By Nicole Drumheller

Nicole Drumheller is a college student of history, works as an aide to handicapped children and is a dedicated dancer of the Tango and the ancient art of Bellydance.

In the spring semester of my college sophomore year, each student in my art class was expected to visit Washington, D.C. to "discover the American spirit" and to express it through our art project.

Upon arriving in Washington, we chose to separate and meet up at the end of the day to share ideas. I had visited the Vietnam Veterans Memorial with my Dad several times, so it was where I decided to wait for an inspiration. I spent a few hours talking to volunteers and passers by.

It wasn't until late afternoon, when I noticed a man who I had seen several times throughout the day. He was sitting on a bench facing the Vietnam Women's Memorial, impassively observing people as they walked from the Wall. His canes were lying on the bench beneath him and his jacket rested across his knees.

I guessed he was a Vietnam Veteran not because he was disabled or the appropriate age, but rather because of his intense presence. His cool stare seemed to reach out to a memory—some distant anger he was struggling to hide. I wanted very much to talk with him, as I had so easily struck up conversations with strangers all day, but I felt intimidated. I thought he needed to be alone. I was about to pass by him when I caught his glance—I knew that this was probably my best chance to meet him so I walked over and introduced myself. He seemed very surprised that I noticed him, and he smiled warmly. We talked for some time about our families, friends, and favorite pastimes, it was as if we were old friends.

As the early signs of dusk reflected in deep red and golden hues from the Wall, the tone of his voice sounded more subdued. I sensed he wanted to speak about the war or the loss of his leg, but he was obviously holding back. I confessed to him I had seen him on several earlier occasions that day and he started to explain why he was there so long, but paused suddenly.

"So you know then? I know where his name is, which panel, which line, the exact location. But I can't bring myself to do it. I'm nothing compared to him, I can't face him, I can't let myself remember, and I certainly can't see my pitiful reflection in that Wall. I'm not ashamed I served in Vietnam. I'm not saying that's why I'm pitiful. I'm pitiful because he should have lived; he deserved to come home; I wish it was me on that damn Wall; it's my place; I inspired his eagerness to be a hero."

I took his hand in mine and held it tightly as he wept.

"I'll go with you if you don't want to go alone." He held my hand tighter and with his other hand touched my face gently. "You're some kind of angel to care about an old man like me. I suppose deep down I was hoping someone would care or at least notice I'm in pain."

I gathered up his canes for him and we silently walked down the path towards the Wall together. He paused and stood still in front of one panel. He didn't say anything to me, he only took my hand and balanced himself in front of the panel. Reaching out carefully with his free hand, he touched the name of the hero he had mentioned earlier. I couldn't read the name, feeling this was his private moment and so I looked away. I stayed with him for support but I knew he needed to see his own reflection alone in the Wall. As he leaned forward to rest his head against the Wall, I turned around to comfort him, tears streaming down his face as he put his arm around me for balance. I cried with him as we walked slowly away from the Wall.

He saw my tears and held me close. "He was my brother you know, and in my mind he's still twenty years old." We both glanced back towards the Wall, as I helped him to a bench. "Why did you take time for me?"

I brushed fresh tears from my eyes as I said, "I respect you for serving in Vietnam. I wanted to make sure you felt welcomed home."

As we parted, he kissed me respectfully on each side of my face. We never exchanged addresses or telephone numbers, but our experience together would bind us forever in spirit. Before he left, he turned round and said, "If you need to remember me, my name is Sean, you can find me forever in the reflection of that Wall, and if you want to remember anyone who has their name on that Wall, just understand the price of freedom and promise us you'll never forget." I watched him as he left, feeling somewhat lost inside. When I met up with students from my art class, I couldn't quite explain my discovery of the American spirit to them, but Sean became more than my art project, he enlightened a part of my soul. In my life—whatever might happen—I will never forget him, or the gift he gave me.

When I went to the Vietnam Veterans Memorial with my parents in seventh grade, I didn't understand why my dad was so touched when he looked at the names. After . . . learning more about what actually happened, I think it is easier to understand.

Mike, age 16

Forgiveness
By Kim Phuc

Kim Phuc is the Good Will Ambassador for UNESCO and heads up her own organization trying to help children around the world who have been hurt in war. This speech was given in 1996 at the Vietnam Veterans Memorial Fund's annual Veterans Day Ceremony at the Wall.

JAN SCRUGGS: It is now time for a most historic moment. Joining Norm McDaniel [former prisoner-of-war] in laying a wreath at this Wall is Ms. Kim Phuc. The world remembers Kim Phuc. Kim's village was under attack when a South Vietnamese plane dropped napalm on a Buddhist pagoda where civilians had taken refuge.

Napalm is a very terrible weapon. It burns through the skin down to the bone. The famous photograph of a nine-year old girl running down Highway 1 shows the cruelty and the ugly horror of military conflict. She endured many years of very painful burn therapy. Yet her private war and her longing for freedom continued.

Two years ago, while en route from Moscow, she and her husband sought political asylum in Canada. She has said that if she could talk to the pilot who dropped the napalm on her, she would forgive him. In that same spirit, today she will lay a wreath alongside Col. McDaniel honoring the U.S. troops who gave their lives.

In this simple gesture, Ms. Phuc has a universal message. She's saying that when wars end we must begin the very difficult process of forgiveness. An innocent victim of war, she feels no anger at the United States.

She feels no anger at the government of Vietnam. She feels no anger at the man who dropped the napalm on her. She was injured. Some of her relatives were killed.

I am pleased to report to you that despite her injuries and despite a very, very difficult life, she is a very charming, vivacious and lively young woman. Her motto is, "Try to keep smiling."

KIM PHUC: Dear friends, I'm very happy to be with you today. I thank you for giving me the opportunity to talk and meet with you on this Veterans Day. As you know, I am the little girl who was running to escape from the napalm fire. I do not want to talk about the war because I cannot change history. I only want you to remember the tragedy of war in order to do things to stop fighting and killing around the world.

I have suffered a lot from the physical and emotional pain. Sometimes I thought I could not live, but God saved my life and gave me faith and hope. Even if I could talk face to face with the pilot who dropped the bombs, I would tell him we cannot change history, but we should try to do good things for the present and for the future to promote peace. I did not think that I could marry, nor have any children because of my burns. But now I have a wonderful husband, a lovely child and a happy family, thank God.

Dear friends, I dream one day people all over the world can live in real peace, no fighting and no hostilities. I should work, we should work, together to be at peace and happiness for all people in all nations. May God bless you.

Vietnam Veterans Today
By Senator John F. Kerry (D-MA)

John Kerry was decorated for heroism as a naval officer in Vietnam. He serves in the U.S. Senate from Massachusetts.

I wonder what most Americans think of today when they hear the words, "Vietnam veteran." Do they first think of the men and women whose names honor the Wall? Do those words bring to mind disabled warriors in VA hospital wards? Or helpless alcoholics and drug addicts living on the streets and in the shelters of our cities? Or might they think of the teachers, doctors, bank presidents, union leaders and ministers who are woven into the fabric of American leadership? I really don't know.

Many lives were forever changed by the Vietnam War. Over 58,000 names of American heroes can be read on the Vietnam Veterans Memorial. Every one of those patriots had a family and friends who still feel that loss. I will never forget a note I read at the exhibit of articles left at the Memorial. A woman's note to her forever 18-year-old boyfriend ended, "I think of you every day." Thirty years later. Every day.

Hundreds of thousands of American servicemen were wounded and even more men and women were emotionally scarred by Vietnam. Many have been unable to live anything that resembles the lives of which they had once dreamed. Their careers, marriages, children and homes also became casualties of their service. So it is— we must always do everything possible to give them hope. Whether it is through counseling or rehabilitation or housing, we must never abandon our veterans in need.

It is absolutely the least we can do and as a senator, one of my most important obligations.

There are many, many Vietnam veterans who served proudly and were able to move beyond the war. More than three million Americans served in Vietnam. Today they are our neighbors, our children's teachers, our physicians, our senators, construction workers, governors, police, firefighters and judges. Many of us learned invaluable lessons in Vietnam about what really matters in this life and have tried to pass on what we learned. For those veterans, the war, although forever an influence, is over.

For other veterans, the war rages on and the battles will never end. But we are all still writing the legacy of that war. We all have opportunities every day to take our experience and make it a positive influence on what we do here and now. We were proud to serve our country 30 years ago. And we still are. Every day.

A Young Girl Grows Up
By Anonymous

This is one of many heartfelt messages sent to the Memorial Fund after people have visited either of our two online sites. Find us at www.vvmf.org or keyword WALL on AOL.

I was used to seeing all the uniforms in San Antonio during the sixties. It seemed that they were as much a part of the scenery around the Alamo as cowboy boots and Stetsons. When I turned 16, my mother who volunteered at the USO, talked me into volunteering as well. I think childhood ended then and there. The uniforms suddenly had names and faces, histories and personalities that I'd never seen before. The accents were from Rhode Island and New Jersey, and fascinating to a Texas girl.

I was still only sixteen when I got my first letters returned from Vietnam, marked KIA and I suddenly realized what those body counts on the evening news really meant.

So many faces still remain in my memory, so many stained letters still lay in my desk, after making their round trip to Vietnam and back into my hands, but I'll never be able to throw them out. Each one is a little piece of my heart that will never be replaced.

No matter who they were, or where they came from, each name on the Wall represents a life unfinished, dreams unrealized, and the loss to us all is without end in this life.

Vietnam: The Illusion
By Alexander M. Haig, Jr.

Alexander Haig, Jr. was White House Chief of Staff under President Nixon, NAO Commander (1974–79), and the Secretary of State under President Ronald Reagan (1981–82). At the start of the Vietnam War, he was Deputy Special Assistant to Secretary Robert McNamara and Battalion and Brigade Commander in the 1st Infantry Division in Vietnam. As Deputy National Security Advisor to President Richard Nixon, he worked to secure the return of U.S. prisoners of war. This is excerpted from his book, Inner Circles, "Chapter 10: Vietnam: The Illusion"

In Vietnam, the United States lost a war that it should and could have won in the name of morality. This grotesque outcome produced the deepest political and moral divisions in the American nation since the Civil War, shook the world's confidence in the leadership of the United States to its foundations, and delivered the unfortunate peoples we had set out to preserve from communism into the hands of a merciless tyranny. How could we have done this to ourselves?

No generally acceptable answer to that question is likely to be furnished by those who fought the war or opposed it. Emotions run too deep, memories linger too vividly, and perceptions of the experience differ in fundamental ways. Perhaps some historian as yet unborn will sort it all out after passions have cooled and consequences have faded away. If this historian of the future happens to be Chinese, he may well describe the American experience in Vietnam as the "Disaster of the Three Mistakes." American policymakers subscribed to the fantasy that the Vietnam War was a civil war, a local event isolated from global issues of ideology and superpower competition; that was the first mistake. They were haunted by the fear that the People's Republic of China, an important supplier of munitions to the Vietnamese Communists, wanted the United States to lose in Vietnam and would even intervene with masses of troops, as in Korea, to guarantee a victory for Hanoi; that was the second mistake. Thirdly, the Presidents who made the war, Kennedy and Johnson, faced with the choice of destroying the enemy or getting out of Vietnam, chose to do neither because they feared that either course would lose them the affection of the American people; that was the greatest mistake of all.

I lived within the conflict quite literally from beginning to end. In the early sixties, as a staff officer in the Pentagon, I witnessed the birth of the Kennedy administration's quixotic delusion that the Communist tide could be turned in Indochina by a combination of covert action, limited unconventional warfare, and the public chastisement and transformation of an embattled and fiercely nationalistic South Vietnamese government into an American-style democracy that would win the hearts and minds of the people. In the Johnson administration, as deputy special assistant to the Secretary of Defense and his deputy, I attended briefings and meetings in which the new President expanded his predecessor's theatrical testing of the theory of counterinsurgency into a calamitous war in which more than 58,000 American military personnel, out of nearly 9 million in uniform, lost their lives. Later on in the Johnson years, from 1966 to 1967, I experienced combat duty. As a member of

President Nixon's staff for national security affairs, and afterward as White House Chief of Staff, I witnessed the agonizing process of American withdrawal. Finally, it was my duty to carry Nixon's messages that notified the last president of independent South Vietnam that the United States had sealed his country's fate by deciding to sign a peace treaty with the North Vietnamese. Everyone suspected Hanoi would never honor this treaty and its credibility depended not only on massive American aid to Saigon but also, ultimately, on the fantasy that the United States would, if necessary, go back. [The reality was that Saigon fell in 1975, two years later.]

We Must Teach Our Children
By James Kimsey

James Kimsey was an Army Airborne Ranger in Vietnam. He is now Chairman Emeritus of America On Line.

The Wall is a sacred site. We all have our own personal, unique experiences and reactions to this Memorial, just as we had our own experiences and reactions to the Vietnam War. But the remarkable and special quality of the Vietnam War and the Memorial is not our differences, but how much we have in common.

We came to this war very young. Different backgrounds. Different races. Different people. And when we returned, we were forever changed. We led our separate lives and we each dealt with the postwar years in our own way. But one thing stayed constant: our respect for each other and the experience we had together. And when this Wall was dedicated we all had another common experience: healing.

The Vietnam Veterans Memorial is truly a wall that heals. On any given day you can witness the healing that takes place on this hallowed ground. This wall was erected to honor the dead, but it also offers hope of healing to the living. There are over 58,000 names inscribed on the Wall. We honor them and our memories of their lives and service. And there are over 40 million people closely related to these names. We must support and honor them, as well.

The Wall has accomplished more than anyone could have dreamed—even Jan Scruggs, and he has a very vivid imagination. It has helped us heal on a personal and national level. It has helped many veterans come to terms with the torment and grief that was kept inside and hidden for so long.

When you first come to the Wall and search for the names of your friends, your comrades, and your family, you see yourself. You see your own reflection in the polished granite and you're forced to realize that easily it could have been you on that Wall, and you can never forget that.

As we celebrate the Wall and all it's accomplished, we realize there is more to be done. Although I don't think anything can have the impact of standing before this Wall and learning the searing effect of the war one name at a time, we must try. There are many people who have not been able to make the journey. So, efforts such as The Wall That Heals, the Memorial Fund's websites and the support groups have reached out to people throughout the country. And now we must engage on our most important outreach program: educating our children about the war.

There are some who have referred to it as the "forgotten war." I reject that. All of you standing here today will make certain the war will not be forgotten.

We will teach our children the lessons we learned as soldiers and as a country, and we will accomplish two goals. We will educate our country's youth and we will heal ourselves. The Vietnam Veterans Memorial Fund is spearheading the efforts to bridge this generational gap.

Many of us who served in the war have witnessed this process in our own families, when our young children began studying the Vietnam War in school and came home with questions. There's nothing like looking in your child's eyes and explaining why and how Daddy went to war. It forces you to confront the issues yourself and it, hopefully, imparts wisdom to your children, so that they can learn from your life lessons.

But many of our country's children know very little, if anything, about the Vietnam War. There's a generational disconnect. We cannot let this happen, not as veterans, not as a nation, and especially with this war where young people played such a role. We were the young men and women fighting in the war, the youngest armed forces the U.S. has ever sent. So, when we embark on our educational outreach to teenagers across the U.S., they will be able to understand. This was not some political battle of old men in a faraway land, these were people almost their own age, faced with difficult choices and incredible challenges; challenges they may have to face someday. They should be ready and we owe it to them to make sure they are.

It has been a long time since we have seen each other. I'll never forget what you did for me and other members of the platoon. When I was lying in the middle of that paddy in an unprotected area near the VC machine gun, I could not believe your bravery when you openly assaulted the VC position. Your taking that hit saved my life and I just simply wanted to say I love you.

Anonymous

Vietnam
By Stanley Karnow

Stanley Karnow, Pulitzer Prize winning author and journalist, covered the Vietnam War. His book, <u>Vietnam: A History</u>, was a PBS Special.

I initially visited Vietnam as a *Time* correspondent in the summer of 1959, and happened to be there on July 8, when a group of guerrillas killed two American military advisers, Major Dale R. Buis and Master Sergeant Chester M. Ovnand, at Bienhoa, a South Vietnamese army base located north of Saigon. My report of their deaths earned only a few paragraphs in the magazine, which was all it deserved. For nobody at that juncture could have imagined that their names would head the list of nearly 60,000 others inscribed on the Vietnam Veterans Memorial in Washington—or that the war that ensued was to claim the lives of two or three million Vietnamese soldiers and civilians. Nor did I dream then that I would go on for the next 16 years to cover the longest conflict—and the first defeat—in U.S. history.

In the period following the fall of Saigon in April 1975, it seemed as if Americans wanted to forget the Vietnam nightmare. As I lecture on the war today, however, I find audiences to be keenly interested in the subject. Older Americans graphically remember the struggle and the acrimonious debates it triggered at home, but many of them are still groping to understand how the nation became involved and what went wrong. Members of the younger generation, most of whom were not yet born when the war ended, have only the vaguest notions about

Vietnam, yet they are eager to learn more. I offer no easy answers, and am myself constantly reexamining the experience in hopes of unearthing fresh information. The effort frequently takes me back to Vietnam to interview the former enemy, a trip currently being made as well by numbers of veterans as they strive for a reconciliation with the men they once fought.

Meanwhile, whether it is viewed in retrospect as a noble cause or a misguided venture, Vietnam has entered our culture, inspiring films, television documentaries, novels and poems. I am astonished that my own book, *Vietnam: A History,* which I reckoned would sink into oblivion following its publication in 1983, has to date sold 1.5 million copies.

In part, the memory of Vietnam summons up in Americans the fear that every fresh troop commitment abroad, be it in Panama, Somalia, the Persian Gulf or Bosnia, could turn into a similar tragedy—or, as the simplistic phrase goes, "another Vietnam." As a result, they have grown cautious and, in contrast to the past, when they assumed that their government never blundered, insist on questioning its decisions. The military, which in my opinion has been wrongly blamed for the Vietnam debacle, shares this prudence. It is healthy, I believe, to the extent that it imposes restraints on the country's political leaders, who now realize that they must consult the public before proceeding into foreign enterprises.

I largely attribute this change to the construction of the Vietnam Veterans Memorial, which has emerged as one of Washington's most popular monuments. Not only does it recognize the sacrifice of those who died in

Southeast Asia, but it also serves as a vivid reminder that the United States cannot afford to act as a global policeman—an illusion of omnipotence promoted by every president since Harry Truman. The world is too small to return to isolationism, yet we should be selective in our engagements.

Vietnam taught us our limitations and that, in a sense, is salutary. But the tuition fee we paid for the lesson—the names on the Wall—was exorbitant.

This Memorial made me feel differently about the war. It made me look at it in a different way. It made me see how many people felt about the war and how much people loved each other. It made me see what an impact on America the war was.

Josh

I Can Only Imagine
By Jennifer Huggins

Jennifer Huggins won a writing competition for high school students, inspired by a visit the Vietnam Veterans Memorial Fund's traveling half scale replica, The Wall That Heals, *made to Atlanta, GA.*

Imagine it is 1965, and while holding your draft letter a tear flows down your cheek. You step out into the adult world only to fear the fate you have been given at age 18. It is now your duty to go serve your country in a war that you know nothing about. However, when your country calls, you must go. The responsibilities you have been given are unthinkable but the job must be done.

It is now 1968, the war is far from over, but at least you have paid your dues and served your time and by the grace of God you have survived this horrid nightmare. At your homecoming all expectancies of a ticker tape parade or at least a hero's welcome only exist in your imagination. While overseas you had no idea of the anger and resentment that was building up for those like you who were sent to fight. This unpopular war was not your choice, but you worked through pain and struggles and watched your buddies give the ultimate sacrifice, only to find that your country not only did not appreciate your efforts, but even loathed all that you stood for. Imagine, ever since you were a young boy you believed that serving your country in uniform was the honorable thing to do. Why then, after your return home, is the acknowledgment and honor normally bestowed upon a veteran so loudly absent? Was it because of the country's regret for losing precious blood in a war that was fought in a way that could not be won?

Our nation's reaction was almost like mass amnesia. If we could forget that this ever happened, then everything would be fine. But the soldiers believed in their government and fought courageously, could we forget that? Monuments are built to remember achievements and the Vietnam War was scarcely that. Even by 1979 when President Carter announced that a memorial to the lives lost during the Vietnam War was to be built, the debate was not settled.

Imagine all the years of pain and yearning to be remembered is finally going to end. Not only does it end, but what once was an issue to be avoided, is put to rest on the most emotional ground in America. Picture the closure as America comes together to build this memorial so precisely and so ingeniously. There are arguments about the color, type and design of this monument, but ultimately the one chosen unanimously displayed simple respect.

As you stand before the Wall and touch the names, you begin to see real people. It is a moving and awe-inspiring experience as those around you search in silence and reverence. The shiny black granite gives a reflection so that you can see yourself in the Wall and think of what these people went through. The Wall reminds, heals, and teaches those who experience it, that this was an important time in history. And although we are not proud of what happened and how those very heroes were treated, we are proud now to honor their lives and mourn their deaths. Their spirits will never be forgotten. The

Wall has become the missing piece to this long, perplexing, and painful part of our history.

Right now I am in the process of losing someone and it made me realize that I should say all I have to say to them while they are still here.

Katie

Vietnam 1968:
Lessons Learned
By General Barry R. McCaffrey

Barry McCaffrey received three Purple Hearts and was twice awarded the Distinguished Service Cross in Vietnam. He led the U.S. Army 24th Infantry Division on the left hook armored assault during Desert Storm. At the time of his retirement, he was an Army Four Star General.

Vietnam in 1968 was a sea of blood. It was the end of innocence. It was the turning point in America's longest war that produced a strategic political defeat with a U.S. casualty toll of 58,000 dead and 303,000 wounded. Three and-a-half million of us served in Southeast Asia with a peak strength of 549,000 troops. We killed more than a million of the communist enemy. In the end, it didn't matter. We got into Vietnam the same way we got out— for all the wrong reasons. But 1968 was the fulcrum on which American national resolve was fractured.

Tet '68 marked the U.S. political-military high tide in Vietnam as surely as the battle of Gettysburg was the high-water mark of the Confederacy. The other side of Tet '68 marked an absolute reversal of U.S. strategic fortunes. Historically, the Tet '68 battle was in many respects a unique military curiosity. U.S. and Allied forces achieved one of the most rapid and lopsided tactical victories in modern warfare. On January 30, 1968, the communist forces opened a massive and brilliantly executed theater-wide surprise attack. Seventy thousand enemy troops launched violent nighttime assaults on more than a hundred population centers. In the subsequent savage combat in cities, the communists lost more than half their forces. Fifty thousand enemy troops were killed in close combat. Most of the casualties were among the local force Viet Cong cadre. By February 4, the communist attack had failed disastrously, although intense fighting continued at Hue and other cities until March. Some two thousand U.S. and four thousand South Vietnamese troops were killed. The stunning military defeat of the communists was compounded by the complete political failure of the expected general uprising among the South Vietnamese people. From 1968 on, the war was principally a North Vietnamese effort characterized increasingly by conventional military tactics.

The courage and daring of American and Allied forces during 1968 was matched by a watershed strategic failure of political will on the U.S. domestic front. The tension between the American press corps and the U.S. military spinmeisters in Saigon flared into open hostility. In the harsh glare of the media spotlight, the American public began to see the lack of purpose in a U.S. military strategy based on mindless defensive employment of enormous firepower. Global condemnation of the ferocious communist terror tactics against helpless captured Vietnamese civilians in Hue and elsewhere could not move an America grown weary of war and contemptuous of the ineffectual and corrupt South Vietnamese regime.

It may well be historically too early to see the 1968 lessons of Vietnam. Harry Summers' brilliant work *On Strategy* has exposed some of the baffling failures of our military strategic thinking. We as a nation have finally started to get beyond simplistic, incorrect explanations. Neither the American media nor U.S. student protests caused us to lose this seven-year struggle. Also, the communists were in the end quite good at war and suppression, but in victory they brutalized the unified nation and then wrecked the economy of Vietnam for a generation. Hundreds of thousands of Vietnamese people fled in desperation on foot through jungles and to death on the sea—something that had never happened in thirty years of French and then American wartime presence. A lot of what Americans thought in 1968 turned out to be dead wrong.

The military turning point of 1968 resulted in a short-term U.S. armed forces buildup that then rapidly evolved into a "Vietnamization" process in which fighting was progressively handed over to the South Vietnamese Armed Forces. In addition, 1968 fundamentally altered the domestic political landscape. A sadly flawed Lyndon Johnson was knocked from presidential office. Tragically, the bad judgment and arrogance of Secretary of Defense Robert McNamara left us on a mind-numbing path of confused strategic purpose that would prolong our bloody losses for another four years until the preponderance of U.S. military power was finally withdrawn.

In retrospect, 1968 in Vietnam was a terrible year. The young men and women of the American armed forces fought effectively and bravely. Sixty percent of those killed were twenty-one years old or younger. We trusted our leaders, our laws, and our parents who had told us that we were expected to serve. We took care of each other. Many of us lost our futures.

Eight million Vietnam-era veterans are now helping run America. Most of us are doing extremely well, although eighty thousand of our combat wounded buddies were severely disabled. Other veterans are traumatized or gutted by drugs and alcohol. The only conclusion that many of us share who served in Vietnam combat during 1968 is that our daughters and sons who are now in uniform deserve better leadership, support, and compassion than we got. Never again.

We Served, Too
By Janis Nark

Janis Nark is a Registered Nurse, author, and 26-year Army veteran with service in Vietnam and Desert Storm. Currently, she is President of her own apparel company, JJ Snow Ltd. and uses her experiences to spread her message that "Change is Mandatory, Stress is Manageable and Misery is Optional."

The first military women to arrive in Vietnam were nurses; it was 1956. As the American presence in Southeast Asia grew, so too did the number of young women who served. In all, nearly 8,000 military women, and thousands more who served in the civilian sector, were there. Eighty three percent of us were nurses; the rest held positions in Special Services, supply, air traffic control, cartography, the USO, American Red Cross and many other jobs in support of our combat troops.

We were all fairly young when we volunteered to serve our country. And many of us were woefully naïve in believing our recruiters' promises; mainly that we could be stationed anywhere in the world that we wanted, and that Vietnam was "strictly voluntary."

Still, when our orders arrived sending us to war, most of us believed in our hearts that we were needed, that what we were doing was important, and that it was our duty to go.

We went to our jobs, faced the perils of enemy fire, horrific heat and humidity, disease, insects, isolation, long work hours and sleepless nights; and then managed to pull ourselves together, dab some perfume behind our ears, and do it all again the next day. We learned a lot about ourselves. We discovered our strengths, and tried to survive our weaknesses. We were ordinary young women trying to function in the most extraordinary of circumstances; dealing in life and death and seeking not just to survive, but to understand.

We did the best that we could with who we were and what we had. And daily, we collected our memories, and stored them away, someplace safe, out of our conscious minds where we thought, "I'll deal with this later."

And after a year we came home, back to "The World." In the span of one plane ride we went from war to peace, from childhood to irrevocable adulthood. We knew we had changed, that our lives would never be the same; and that we could never explain any of it to the folks back home.

We couldn't and we didn't. For as unacceptable as it was for the guys to talk about the war when they came home . . . *no one* wanted to acknowledge that young women had been there. Even as Women's Lib was making its voice heard, the underlying message was clear: nice girls wouldn't have gone to war.

We came home quietly, went back to our homes, our families, our jobs; and never spoke about the war to anybody. Many of us quit nursing, and never knew why. Some of us had recurring nightmares, flashbacks, unexplained illnesses, depression, or abused drugs or alcohol. Many women applied themselves with a fury to school . . . attaining one degree after another, to work . . . rising to the top leadership positions in their companies, their churches, their social organizations, their families . . . anything to avoid the memories they had stored away "to think about later." The memories had created a deep impenetrable wound that needed to be healed.

In 1982, the initial healing ground was laid, in the form of the Vietnam Veterans Memorial—the Wall. The women, just like men who served, were drawn to it. The healing power of that sacred place is evident to all that have been there. We could go to the Wall, and mourn, and cry, and reach out for comfort if we chose...and yet it was so easy to be invisible there. Women simply weren't recognized as veterans.

Veterans Day 1993, the Vietnam Women's Memorial is dedicated in Washington, D.C. Thousands of us vets attend and we are overwhelmed. We lead the parade . . . the nurses, Red Cross workers, entertainers, women who worked in administration, logistics, and intelligence. The streets are lined with people applauding and crying. A vet sits high up in a tree yelling, "Thank you! Thank you!" A man in a flight suit stands for over two hours at attention, saluting as the women pass by. People hand us flowers and hug us. One GI has a picture of his nurse taken "July 1964." He is trying to find her.

We find each other. We know, at last, that we are not alone, that we are not crazy or paranoid, but that we have a lot of work to do in order to heal. We talk to each other and find comfort as well as pain in our words, and our tears. Words and tears that now, finally we share. Now, after so many years, the process has finally begun . . . and we hold each other close, and say, "Welcome home!"

It's been said that our generation can't even begin to comprehend what it's like to live during a time of war . . . but I will leave this Memorial with a different outlook, one of appreciation for a life of peace.

Susan

A Tribute to the Gold Star Mothers and Fathers
By Lewis W. Hosler

Lewis Hosler served three tours in Vietnam with the 1st and 9th Infantry Divisions. He wrote this in honor of the parents of all the men and women whose names are on the Wall.

Though often asked how it was to live,
In jungles fighting every day,
Sometimes the truth just hurts too much,
We must be careful what we say,
We buried a Gold Star Mother this very day

The fathers so very proud of their brave sons,
Forever knowing they could be the ones
Whose names are inscribed upon this wall of stone,
Never again to see their families, home.

Our only hope is that America learns,
Before brave soldiers take their turn,
The cost and price that we must pay,
To protect our freedom each and every day.

Should someday in heaven we would meet
All together without retreat,
Parents and sons may each we seek,
To greet them all and shake their hands,
For a job well done in that faraway land.

In spirit the parents will always be,
Both in our hearts for eternity.
They gave their sons so we could live,
All they had, their lives to give.
They gave their lives in freedom's name,
They gave their all, and we feel their pain.
Never their lives to be the same.

I can't imagine what it must feel like to see a name of someone you love . . . up on this Wall. What courage it takes to stand and look and reach out and touch the letters . . . as if touching his face once again.

Valerie

A High Price To Pay
Dr. Elaine Niggemann

After returning from her service in Vietnam as a nurse with the 24th Evac Hospital, Elaine Niggemann attended medical school and is now a practicing cardiologist in Scottsdale, Arizona.

When I went to Vietnam as an Army nurse less than a year out of college, the thought of a Vietnam Women's Memorial would have been beyond my wildest imagination. Although I felt very wise and mature, in retrospect, I was really fairly young, very naïve, and sometimes foolish. When I returned, I was, of course, a year older, much more mature, and certainly wiser. The wisdom I gained in Vietnam has continued to grow and mature with time, changing perspectives, and life's experiences, especially becoming a physician and a mother.

The Vietnam Women's Memorial is meaningful to me, to the women who served during or in Vietnam, and to our country. First, it is a tribute and recognizes those women who served. We worked hard, we cared, and we sometimes cried. I remember many of my patients. I remember their names, faces, hometowns, wounds and injuries, and sometimes their deaths.

Much has been written and said about the physical and emotional trauma of Vietnam. There were, however, positive aspects of the experience. My time in Vietnam was enlightening and growth producing, to say the least. I acquired excellent nursing experience and assumed more responsibility than if I had remained in a stateside civilian nursing position.

More important than the professional growth was the personal growth. I discovered that despite our problems here in America, we are really very fortunate to live in a country with the freedom and opportunities we enjoy. I discovered the thrill of travel to foreign countries and experiencing new cultures, just like my recruiter promised.

As I met the daily challenges of my work in Vietnam, I discovered a sense of self-confidence and the value of perseverance. Later in life, during some of the more demanding periods of medical school and residency, I sometimes found myself thinking, "If I can get through Vietnam, I can do this."

It was also in Vietnam that I discovered the fragility of human life. Our tenuous physical existence continues to hold me in awe.

Finally, I discovered the satisfaction of being able to make a difference by doing the best I could and caring. It was a year filled with many discoveries. And although I didn't appreciate it at the time, it had a major impact on my life. I am truly grateful for the opportunity to have served in Vietnam as an Army nurse. I am proud of my contribution. I know that the doctors, nurses, corpsmen, medevac helicopter pilots, Red Cross, and all those involved in the military and medical care made a difference.

When my three-year old and five-year-old sons visit this Memorial some day, I want them to be proud of their mom. I think they will be—the Women's Memorial is a beautiful tribute to the women who served in recognition of hard work, devotion, and a willingness to give of themselves. I also believe the Vietnam Women's

Memorial, like the Wall, is a reminder to our country of the lessons we learned.

We all know that peace and freedom have a high price. In the Vietnam Women's Memorial, a wounded soldier is held in the arms of a nurse. I would go back and be the nurse, but I don't ever want one of my sons to be that soldier. We did learn lessons in Vietnam. Let's remember them and let there be no more Walls.

We remember. And when we are gone, the Wall shall speak for us, saying "No more!"

Unattributed

Will Our Next War Be On The Web?
By Peter S. Prichard

Peter Prichard is President of The Freedom Forum, a nonpartisan foundation that helps the public and the media understand one another better, as well as the President of the Forum's Newseum. From 1988 through 1994, he was editor-in-chief of USA Today.

"The first casualty when war comes is truth."
—U.S. Senator Hiram Johnson, 1917

In 1968, I was a young enlisted man in the Mekong Delta, serving as an intelligence "advisor" to the South Vietnamese Army. In Can Tho, the Delta's regional headquarters, the hundreds of coordinated attacks by the Viet Cong across the country the night of January 30 seemed to take our officers by surprise. A report of hundreds of sampans moving down the Bassac River "in formation" broke the sleepy spell of the Tet holiday; the mortars and fierce firefights at Vinh Long Airport that night concentrated everyone's minds.

The Tet Offensive proved to be a serious military defeat for the Communist forces, but it was a huge psychological victory. Scenes on American television showing U.S. paratroopers reclaiming the U.S. Embassy from a band of suicidal sappers extinguished "the light at the end of the tunnel"—and Lyndon Johnson's presidency.

Tired of promises their leaders did not keep, mired in an unpopular struggle against a determined enemy in a strange and distant land, Americans' protests rose and a long and difficult withdrawal began. Today we have 58,000 names on a black granite Wall to remind us of the pain.

If we were at war today, would we see similar scenes? Would the correspondents of the world's media be allowed to roam the battleground to report what they saw and heard?

Not likely. As Grenada and the Gulf War showed, military management of the media is a high priority of today's Pentagon. Vietnam was probably the last war where correspondents had easy access to the fighting. These brave reporters and photographers—Peter Arnett, Tim Page, Horst Faas, Tad Bartimus, Bernard Fall, David Halberstam, Dickey Chappelle and many others— walked where the grunts walked, hid in the same ditches, dodged the same bullets. Many, like Chappelle and Fall, died there. They risked or even lost their lives to bring the world a record of the Vietnam War: the victories and the defeats, the valor and the folly.

Contrast that open access with the leashed reporters of the Gulf War—the war where hundreds of correspondents were corralled in a Saudi briefing room, where they were spoon fed news nuggets by field-grade spinmeisters.

What do we know today of the exploits of the coalition's Special Forces behind Sadam's lines, in their dune buggies? Did we really see the reality of the air war? How accurate were our "smart" bombs? Did the Patriot missiles really knock down Scuds? What killed the Israeli civilians, the Scuds or our countermeasures?

All are legitimate questions and some of which our capable military is still trying to answer. Maybe they will, maybe they won't. Or maybe next time the Pentagon will post its briefings on the web and ask the reporters to click away. Some media companies might even welcome the travel savings.

In Vietnam, thanks to the easy access the military gave the media, at least we had a lot of information. Some of it was false, but it was all there. As a soldier whose life was at stake, I appreciated every bit of it. And the American people, who are hard to fool in the long run, watched it and read it and listened to it and made up their minds.

That's how democracy works—the worst system except for all the others—and is supposed to work. In Vietnam, truth was not the first casualty of war reporting. The first casualty was just a metaphor—the one about the tunnel.

Part of the Wall
By Harry Robinson

Harry Robinson was wounded in Vietnam. He is a practicing architect and Vice President of Howard University in Washington, DC. He volunteers his time for a number of charitable causes, including the Memorial Fund's Board of Directors.

Each of us has come to remember and reflect, to once again commune this Veterans Day as comrades-in-arms with those who supported us, to remember our bonds of friendship and ties of family in the service of this great democracy, and to reflect upon the meaning of sacrifice, our sacrifice, the ultimate sacrifice of those whose names bring high honor to all veterans.

We have come with a sense of voice, a sense of place, and a sense of time.

Our voice, as it did when we fought and returned from our war, speaks the language of a very special generation instilled with an idealism that is undeterred by other voices speaking slightly of our spirit and contribution. It is a voice spoken from the Wall's pristine black granite face. It is a voice whose resonance brings clarity and reason to the national discourse on "fighting to win rather than fighting not to lose." It is a voice that will span generational transitions, enduring forever in this nation's memory. It is an impassioned voice, speaking to children, parents and grandparents yet unborn on the meaning of war, its causes, purposes and results. It is an important and essential voice. It is our voice, our nation's voice.

We have come with a sense of place to this site of healing and life. Our healing place which resides in the national conscience with ever increasing insistence, yet with patience and understanding. This place which has evolved its own personality. We come on a pilgrimage to this place of sacrament and we are embraced by her healing panels and gently sloping land. This place possessing so many hopes and memories and so much faith. Remembering and reflecting, the people come to this place, our Wall. She is broad enough in her love to share her powers with all who come to her. She absorbs our grief and wipes tears. She is the eternal keeper of our legacy. In her mystical way, she has closed the wounds of armed conflict abroad and public strife on our native shores. This place, our place, our Wall. We come with a sense of place.

We also come with a sense of time. Every voice and place exist within the frame of time. Our time, the time of our voice and of this place are without limits and exist as one. Time can neither erode nor otherwise diminish this union of spirit and purpose. The strength of the images of our time continues to develop and influence where this nation finds itself today and in the future.

We come with a voice, a sense of place and a sense of time. In ten years, 25 million of us have come. As we come, we discover that we belong to the family of all who have come before and all who will come after. And that we are drawn to return and return again. We become part of the Wall and the Wall becomes part of us. We and the Wall are one. Inseparable. We come to this altar, this threshold between the past, the present, the future. And each time we leave more whole, more healed. More centered.

On behalf of the Memorial Fund, I welcome you to

come to the Wall again and again. I thank you for your voice, your sense of place and your sense of time as you become one with the Vietnam Veterans Memorial.

As I looked at the names on the Wall, I was touched, and happy because my daddy, a Vietnam veteran, is not on it. Love and peace to all of the families with friends and family on the Wall.

Kari

The Stories Must Be Told
By Governor Tom Ridge

Tom Ridge was an infantry sergeant in Vietnam. After serving in the U.S. Congress, he is now the Governor of Pennsylvania.

I was a 22-year old working class kid when I was drafted into the Army to serve in Vietnam. I was proud to serve my country and proud to serve with many of you as a grunt.

I'm proud to have worn my country's uniform and I'm proud to have served side-by-side with men who fought for the cause of freedom, and the women whose care and courage helped many of our comrades through the darkest of hours and the longest of days.

Each generation has a story to tell, stories which unite one generation to the next. From generation to generation, the story is the same, retold in different places, in different ways, but always an ode to liberty sung by families who have consecrated the democratic ideals of liberty and justice with their suffering, their blood, and their lives. That is the legacy; the call to duty and sacrifice in the name of freedom that we, as young men and women who came of age in the sixties, inherited from our fathers, just as they had from their fathers before them.

Much has been made of the differences between the war we fought and the wars fought by our fathers. The gulf that lies between us is more imagined than real. For those who experienced combat, those who have been immersed in the soul-searing, white heat of war, the distinctions of time and place are ephemeral. We share an eternal kinship with all who come before us and all who come after. It's a sacred bond that's born of shared adversity, shared suffering and shared sacrifice. Same mud, same blood.

I remember a boyhood friend—and we all have similar memories—who answered the call to serve. When our fathers met after the war, they both talked with pride about our service, but his dad's words were filled with pain. My friend was scheduled to come home. He was out of the field, standing down, waiting for the bird to take him back to the world. But when his comrades came under attack, he insisted on going back out. His last mission proved to be just that, but his deeds of heroism live on in the lives of his fellow soldiers who survived.

For this and countless other examples of heroic self-sacrifice and courage, those who have survived must tell their story. And if it weren't for the heroes on the Wall, many of us would not be here today. So it is with heartfelt respect, with love and the blessings of God that we say to each and every one of them, "Thank you."

Standing Vigil
By James Miller

James Miller is one of the high school winners of an Atlanta writing contest during the visit of The Wall That Heals.

Walking along the mall on a hot summer day, I was tired. I had been in Washington for a week now, and had toured many significant historical sites. The Vietnam Veterans Memorial came next on our agenda: a tour tacked onto the end of a long day. I knew very little about the conflict, except that my grandfather had been a quartermaster over there for a couple of years.

As we neared the Wall, I noticed a flagstaff and a statue with soldiers. I thought, with a roll of my eyes, "Here we go again." I then turned and beheld the Wall. The majestic polished black granite reflected the bright sunlight and the faces of throngs of people. I started down the path, and an eerie silence filled the air. I noticed the many items that had been left: a child's letter to her grandfather, combat decorations, a solitary rose. I personally knew no one whose name is on the Wall, yet as I looked at just a handful of the over 58,000 names inscribed on the Wall, a deep sense of sorrow flooded over me. The Wall had left its mark on my soul.

The Wall stirs the emotions in everyone who visits. It powerfully says things that no statue can even begin to say. While I stood there reading those names, seeing my own face reflected in the granite the conflict seemed something very real to me. Something this nation should never forget. The Wall now serves as a daily reminder of past mistakes while forcing conversations on the delicate subject of the war. The effect it conveys, whether that of grief or happiness, can be viewed only in a positive light.

For the veterans, the Wall heals the gaping wound left in their soul since their return to a hostile society. There they remember the times they shared with fallen comrades. The experience of war forever changes the men and women who fight, and the Wall works as a connecting symbol to which veterans can turn. This is an important function since it gives the veterans some form of unifying identity: something due to them since they returned to scorn in America after war's end.

For the relatives and friends of those who lost their lives in Vietnam, the Wall serves as a healing wall, just as it does for veterans. For the rest of our society, especially the younger generations, the Wall serves less as a healing wall but rather functions as a reminder of the consequences of war. Whether the Vietnam War should have been fought or not, the fact remains that over 58,000 people died in the jungles of Vietnam thousands of miles from home. The Wall honors these brave men and women who died for their country, and forces contemplation on why our country goes to war. Perhaps most importantly, the Wall stands vigil in Washington as a constant reminder of that dark era in our nation's history. For if we forget our past mistakes, they will certainly happen again.

This message is for the families and the veterans that went to Vietnam. It is so sad just to think of all the lives that were lost, all the dreams that were broken, all the tears that we are still crying from those heroes that will never come back home. This is from my heart.

If you are able save for them a
Place inside of you
And save one backward glance
When you are leaving for the
Places they can no longer go.
Be not ashamed to say you love
Them and that you will never forget
Them. For each time you mention
Their names and remember them
They are finally being honored and
Respected like the real heroes
Each and all of them are.
And finally with a big smile all
Of them can say we truly are
Home.

Unattributed

The Spirit of the Wall
By Laurence A. White

Laurence White served in Vietnam in 1969–1971 and presented another poem at the 1992 Concert commemorating the 10th Anniversary of the Wall.

These lonely thoughts of war we dread
Are haunted by the souls of dead;
Who stand among the shadows where
They look with cold judgmental stares.
What is it in their glance we see
That they would want from you or me?
A moment's past decision then
Had cost the lives of many men,
And left us with such guilt to bear
Beneath our own condemning stares.

The years ahead may not be kind
Because of those we left behind.
The fact that we came home again
Has left us little peace within,
And so around us we have built
The Walls we mortared without guilt;
That seem to darken evermore
The light of hope we had before.

We look for answers but find doubt;
Uncertain then what life's about;
Perhaps regretting after all
Our names weren't written on the Wall.

And so we ask the question, "Why?
Some men live while others die?"
And find no long enduring peace
When endless battles never cease,
Where we condemn ourselves because
We could not change the way it was.

  The question always seems to be,
  "What is our course in destiny?"

We know someday we'll join them there,
Among the shadows where they stare,
And then we'll have to face each one
Explain to them what wasn't done
And why we simply did not taste
Life's fullest cup, we chose to waste,
While dying men with trembling lips,
Had been denied just one more sip.

  So if they had the chance to give
  Would they have had the will to live?
  Or would they ask the question, "Why?

Some men live while others die?"
There is no way that we can see
The right or wrong of what could be.
So if our names exchanged with them
It would not change what happened then,
For no one knows where futures lie
Except, that someday, we will die.

The lives we live must then create
A deeper meaning for their fates,
Or else the guilt we wear inside
Will haunt forever 'til we've died.
The death of those succumbing first
Should not deny the lives we thirst,
But rather savor from the vine
Each day for them, life's sweetest wine.

We are their living legacy,
The last of mortal breath to be,
That speak about what happened then
So it will not occur again.
We must not carry such a load
So let the walls of guilt erode,
Accept the fact that we should "live"
And then perhaps ourselves forgive,
And truly live their legacy
Denying death its victory.

> *We cannot let the years slip by*
> *In search of answers to the "Why?"*
> *For time and tide will wait for none*
> *Then suddenly our journey's done.*
> *And so without lifelong regret*
> *We do not owe death any debt,*
> *Except to be, then after all,*
> *The Living Spirit of the Wall.*

Miracles of Healing
By Father Philip Salois, M.S.

Philip Salois was a rifleman in Vietnam. He is now a Catholic priest, and affiliated with the National Conference of Viet Nam Veteran Ministers. He gave this prayer in 1992.

In 1982, when the Vietnam Veterans Memorial was dedicated, the chaplain began his invocation with these words: "Your presence here is felt like a mighty wind, oh Lord." As we commemorate years of healing engendered by this Memorial, we have observed and indeed experienced firsthand that the mighty wind was the very breath of God.

As human faith in God has been transfigured over and over again in the mirrored images of the men, women, and children who through their veil of tears and amid their pain and sorrow have sought and received comfort, consolation and inner peace. Let us pray:

All powerful God, your eternal promise of never forgetting one of your children has generated countless miracles of healing here at the Vietnam Veterans Memorial. You have indeed consecrated this ground as holy. You have used this instrument as a visible means to speak to the hearts and souls of all whom have come here seeking forgiveness, reconciliation and resolution in their lives.

Remember them, oh Lord, the gift of light and sacrifice these men and women of Vietnam have offered. For them we give you thanks. Remember also, those men whose fate is known to you alone. Bless them and us for the mystery to be revealed. Remember finally the holy remnant of war, those who wear their scars visibly or secretly. Grant them and us freedom from enslavement and freedom for light. Amen

---

You are missed . . . almost 30 years later . . . you are thought of often by all of us that you left behind . . . your life and your death, one of our greatest joys was to know you and one of life's great sorrows was to lose you so early.

Your friends from the class of 1966

White Gloves
By Mary Anne Russell

Mary Anne Russell attended high school with Robert Bagnall, whose name can be located at Panel 34 East, line 40. She has published several poems, and lives with her family in Sevierville, Tennessee.

Mother paged through the names,
    In the book of names,
    And then, businesslike
    read aloud,
     "Robert S. Bagnall,
    Bloomfield, Connecticut."
    And I read too, but silently,
    Remembering
    High school basketball
    And yearbook photos.
    "January, 1968—
    Date of Casualty," it said.
    Impersonal words for death.
    "Row 34E," she said
    and stiffened,
"Line 40," she said, and turned away
as it struck.
"I will not cry," I thought,
Remembering
A boy I hardly knew,
We all admired,
Healthy, handsome, easygoing,
Clean cut.
His hands in such white gloves, folded.

Brass buttons. Navy blue linen.
"I will not laugh," I thought,
> *thirty years ago,*
> *teenage cool at the funeral.*
But ambushed by those stilled gloved hands,
I sobbed like a child,
And reached to his own mother for comfort.

Our safe young lives.
> *Bobby had it planned so well*
> *In his good and easy way—*
> *Team captain, class president,*
> *High school graduate,*
> *Soldier,*
> *College,*
> *Career.*
Exploded, they said.
Was it a quick clean cut
> *Or did he suffer?*
> *Was he alone*
> *Or did he die among friends?*

The Wall was only one inch high
> *At first.*
> *And then a name.*
> *And then three names,*
> *Then five.*
> *Then I stopped counting.*

I took a photograph where the Wall
> *Towered like an ancient obelisk,*
> *Monument to some dark mystery.*

A woman dabbed her eyes,
  Looking at a brother, a cousin,
  A son,
  Forever young.
His name
  Next to so many other names—
  His friends?
  Or soldiers dying in another place
  In the same hour?
  Question upon question.

We saw ourselves reflected, ghostlike,
  Otherworldly
  In the Wall
  Against the names,
Solid names carved in granite.
We reached out from our pool of reflections
And touched the names,
Wanting something.
  Who were these boys, these men?
  Why had they died?
  A thousand million reasons
  Beyond us now,
  Within us forever.

A Life Remembered
By Gene Fry

Gene Fry served in Vietnam and only made it to the Wall in 1998. This is excerpted from a piece he produced to help other vets. He plans to include it in his forthcoming book with a working title of War—More Than Blood and Guts.

Standing before my brothers and sisters memorialized on this Wall, I feel embarrassed and unworthy. Trained to show no pain, to never complain, and to be prepared to give the last full measure in unselfish sacrifice, I am ashamed to seek help for the emotional pain I incurred in the battles that took their lives. I have lived these past three decades, albeit with numerous disabilities and constant physical pain, while so many have slept, wrapped in the darkness of their suddenly arrested youth. I have walked across spring meadows and rustled in the fall leaves on two legs; I have held my children with two capable arms; I have seen a thousand sunsets with two appreciative eyes. Too many of those who fought beside me came home maimed in body far beyond the wounds I incurred. So why do I still feel such pain?

I know some that have ended their lives. One is Greg, one of my best friends. He was a brave soldier, an affectionate friend, and a good son. Christmas 1997 has come and gone, and for these weeks I have been thinking a lot about my friend, Greg. He was 16 months older than I, and stood 6'6" tall. We were teenagers together, becoming young men destined to have much of our youth taken from us by war. But before that we double-dated and hung out together. We even worked at the same store, until our country redirected our lives. We lost contact when we went off to war; I ended up with the 101st Airborne Division, he was with the 4th Infantry Division.

We both served during the Tet offensive, 1967–68; many of the men in my unit were wounded or killed. I ask myself, why did I not die? That question haunts me to this day. I came home with injuries, some paralysis, but basically in one piece. My friend Greg served a full year without a scratch and I always joked with him because he was so big and such a good target. I knew his parents well, and when Greg got home his mom called me and asked if I would come over to see him. She said he was not himself. I understood this, because neither was I. She asked me to come as soon as possible, which I did. When I saw Greg, we hugged one another and were exceptionally close for a while, going everywhere together. Many times during the day we would drink enough to lower our shields. Then we cried together— recounting stories in fragments, the other nodding and filling in the gaps—and then cried again. I am not sure how long Greg was home, but I think it was around two months. One day, 30 years ago, Greg took his life by hanging himself in the basement of his home. I remember the phone call from his mother as she tried to keep back the tears and anger. To this day I think of Greg often. I loved him, and I miss him. Sometimes, I hate him for doing this to me. Still, I have forgiven him because I know exactly how he felt. I see his face now, only days before his death, and remember him crying in a parking lot. He was screaming, "Why?" Obviously, the pain was so great that he could not handle it, and I was too young to understand or know how to get help for him. In fact, I just started getting help for myself. One more fallen soldier; one more sacrifice to a war; but his name did not make it to the Wall.

I am now 50 years old and feel the same as I did in those early days following combat. I still have the same feelings, I still try to deal with them, and I still wonder why. I know this is a large burden vets drag to the Wall, the Wall that represents our comrades who have died or are still Missing In Action. I hope and pray that no more soldiers commit suicide for something they were drafted to do, and guided or forced into. I understand the feeling of betrayal. I vehemently plead with other veterans to live, to reach others in spite of their own pain. Stay alive to give honor to those who have fallen.

A Visit to the Wall
By Charles B. Wilson

Chuck Wilson is a Vietnam veteran and worked with the Vietnam Veterans Leadership Program in New York to help house and rehabilitate veterans in need of help.

As my wife, Sherry, and I walked the length of the Washington Mall from the Capitol toward the Lincoln Memorial, school bus after school bus opened their doors and released their captive riders into the sunny, 84-degree day. The air was filled with the raucous sounds of youth, sounds of traffic and noontime joggers and thousands of tourists frantically trying to see all they possibly could in their allotted time in the nation's capital.

In town to attend the annual conference of the National Coalition for Homeless Veterans, Sherry and I finally were able to visit the Vietnam Veterans Memorial, a pilgrimage I had steadfastly avoided until now.

Drinking in the sights and sounds of a warm May afternoon in DC, a new sensation seized me as we drew within 300 yards of the as-yet-unseen Wall. A reverential silence replaced the sounds to which I had become accustomed on the walk and the feeling was almost eerie.

In a few short moments, we saw the Memorial. Despite the fact that over 100 people were present, it was a completely silent scene. A scene which caused a wave of sorrow to envelop me like a shroud. Tears welled in my eyes at the realization of the Wall. I glanced at Sherry, almost embarrassed by my tears and saw the same thing on her face. With a husband and brother who had served and come home again, the impact of over 58,000 names inscribed on the Wall was as moving to her as it was to me.

As we approached, the silence was replaced (at least in my subconscious mind) by the sounds of gunfire, explosions, the smell of cordite and blood, and the screams of good young men who would not come home again. In seconds, I saw faces, remembered names long forgotten until this moment. I again saw the laughing bravado that could not cover the underlying sheer terror felt by all of us. I became angry at the waste of America's youth in a land so far away.

Sorrow rushed in to replace the anger. Sorrow that so many mothers' babies, good women's husbands and babies' fathers had sacrificed their lives in Southeast Asia for a cause they did not fully understand in a conflict that few supported at home.

The sorrow was accompanied by a powerful, irrational guilt. Guilt that I had come home when so many fine young men with such bright futures saw their dreams, hopes and expectations violently ripped apart when Death visited them in a foreign place. A place that they really didn't know or understand. A guilt that I had not come to talk to them, to say goodbye, to tell them how much I loved each and every one of them sooner—I simply couldn't do it.

As I stared at the Wall (I could not make myself look for names known to me in that earlier life—and there are many), the noises of conflict, screams of agony and sounds of war faded into the mists and were replaced by fleeting images of young, smiling, boyish faces. Faces filed with peace, understanding and forgiveness.

A short distance from the Wall, Sherry and I sat on a

bench while the waves of emotion swept over us. As if in one voice, gentle and kind, every voice of every person on the Wall was telling me, "It's okay. It's over. All of us are at peace and that is what we wish for you. Thanks for coming. Remember us with love, accept, forget and forgive."

"It's over."

My tears of sorrow were replaced by tears of release. After all those years of torture and torment, I finally found closure. With that closure, so magnificently granted by the people whose names are on the Wall and that gorgeous day in Washington, came something I have been looking for—for such a very long time—inner peace and gratitude that I had known and will always remember young men as fine as these.

Remembering Jim
By Cindy Alloway

Cindy Alloway's brother, James Ardon Alloway, served in Vietnam from September 1968 to June 1969. He was honored in the In Memory *program, which is dedicated to those Vietnam veterans who die prematurely from causes related to the war, such as PTSD-induced suicides or Agent Orange cancer. She gave this speech at the most recent In Memory Program.*

My brother, Jim, was 19 years old when he was sent to Vietnam to serve in the demilitarized zone with the Seabees. When he left Iowa, he was excited to go help save the people of Vietnam who were being oppressed. He was going as a liberator with righteousness. Like all his comrades, he was going to give his best for his country. It was an adventure and he had a perpetually positive spirit about him.

We aren't exactly sure how or when my brother returned to the U.S. My parents received a call from the Naval Hospital in Michigan that he was there. When we arrived, we were told he had been diagnosed as 100% mentally disabled and given an honorable discharge. His compassionate hopeful brain could no longer make any sense out of the illogical events he experienced during the war. He had become poor in spirit.

When Jim was discharged from the hospital, he wanted to give speeches to tell people the details of the war so we could all learn from what he experienced. He said, "You never really understand it until you are in the middle of it." Jim was not angry at our government. He was just scared for the rest of us that this kind of tragedy might happen again. He wanted us to understand how good we had it, so safe, so far away from war.

My original brother never came back from Vietnam. But we accepted, loved and worked with what was left of him. When he was taking his medicine, Jim was able to keep a job, get married, and have a son, Kirk. But the side effects of his medicine bothered him so much he would stop taking it. During one of those tumultuous times, after he was divorced and awaiting bed space in a VA inpatient psychiatric hospital to open up, he decided he had had enough suffering and took his own life.

It is hard for family members when someone dies this way. It was especially hard on his son, Kirk, who had never really understood how Vietnam had affected his Dad until he came to the In Memory ceremony three years ago, when he was 17 years old.

When Kirk saw the memorial displays lined up honoring others like his Dad's and heard people speak about their experiences, he finally had an understanding of what his father had fought for and suffered. Instead of shame and guilt about his Dad's problems, this ceremony gave him a sense of pride for his father that nothing else had ever done before. When we walked along the Wall after the ceremony, he saw three men with hats on with the Seabees insignia on them. He went up to them and told them about his father. They immediately told him what it was like to work with the Seabees in Vietnam and adopted him as an extended family member. They hugged him and exchanged addresses. My nephew, Kirk, has a whole new perspective and my whole family is very grateful for all the healing that occurred that Veteran's Day, three years ago.

My brother, Jim, was always thinking about the other guy. He would want us to reach out to those who are the "walking wounded" today. It is never too late to help our other brothers and sisters who are still with us. That is why I think it is so important to support ceremonies like the In Memory ceremony and reach out to each other while we are together.

The Wall speaks for itself. Anything that anyone could possibly say no matter how eloquent would only pale in comparison.

Unattributed

Combat Veteran
By Rod Kane

Rod Kane served in the Central Highlands, Vietnam, 1965–66, as an airborne medic in infantry. He fought in the Ia Drang Valley, some of which is recounted in his book, <u>Veterans Day</u>.

I went down to the Wall the other day, with a friend. I never go down alone. The area was sparsely populated and peaceful, especially since they removed the pack rats selling t-shirts. I went to the bottom 2nd panel and revisited my first ambush, as I've done many times before and SLAM! It hits me. Again. Not like I hadn't already seen it for myself many times and had the theory behind it explained but SLAM! It hits me every time.

The names.

First names, middle initials, last names. The names were unadorned by rank—no Captains, Colonels, PFCs, just names. Just men, just women. Just names. These people with their names on the Wall had nothing left to prove and they didn't need trumped up rivalries to make them feel useful.

It brought back to me the contests we would hold amongst ourselves as to "who was best, who did the most, who had the worst luck, who was killed while sleeping in his bunk . . ." Vying for win, place or show. Maybe it's human nature, and it has always been this way.

"We did this better, no one else knows because they weren't there . . ." A badge of war. A badge of courage. And if we were massacred, all the better. We hold these jousts not only amongst ourselves—we compete against the old guys, the other wars, too. Vietnam gets in there and vies with the Big One, WWII, The Frozen Chosen, Little Big Horn. Does it make sense? Why jockey for a position in hell?

So I don't identify myself as a Vietnam veteran any more. Not because I'm not proud of serving in Vietnam. Hell, I was a Vietnam veteran when Vietnam vets weren't cool. But you know what, folks? In the end, I'm just a combat veteran. Who had it better? Who had it worse? By our deeds we shall be known. We all share the title.

Combat veteran, that's all.

That's enough.

Looking at the Wall and the offerings left there makes me realize how precious life is and how death can affect people. Vietnam is one war of which I don't think I'll ever quite grasp the full pain. Looking at the picture of all "our boys" makes me think of my cousins, my favorite of which died from the effects of Agent Orange years after he returned home.

Unattributed

Teach The Children Well
By Stephen Sossaman

Stephen Sossaman served in the 9th Infantry Division artillery in the Mekong Delta. He is now a professor of English at Westfield State College in Massachusetts, and the trainer for the Veterans Education project in Amherst, MA. He is currently working with the Memorial Fund to help bring the tools of his veteran outreach program to schools across the nation.

The Vietnam Veterans Memorial has proven to be far more powerful and important than anyone could have ever imagined. One source of its power is its inclusion of names, an insistence on the humanity of every individual counted among the dead.

Each of those names represents a unique individual with a unique set of life experiences. Many of their stories are lost to us now outside of the memories of their families and their comrades.

Living veterans, on the other hand, have an extraordinary opportunity to share their stories with others, especially the nation's young people. Perhaps in years past, few wanted to listen, and few were prepared to understand, but that dark period is over.

Since then some of us have discovered that sharing our most meaningful experiences is our most powerful tool for achieving not only self understanding and reconciliation, but also for making a meaningful contribution towards the maturation and character development of young people.

The Veterans Education Project in Amherst, MA, has trained veterans since 1982 to understand the most meaningful moments of their military service, to craft those true stories into powerful oral history narratives, and to tell them in classrooms and youth programs in our area.

Young people have proven surprisingly eager to hear what we have to say. They know little about the war, and about the experiences of individual veterans, but like all human beings they respond instinctively and positively to stories.

Veterans can counteract this abuse and neglect of the nation's young by telling their own stories, frankly and unselfishly. This can be painful, because the stories we tell are true and the lessons we learn are not always flattering and comforting. Many of our most powerful stories come from incidents when we faltered, or chose wrong, or failed to act wisely, or discovered an unpleasant truth. Still, these stories must be told.

Many psychologists tell us that the human love of stories is rooted in our tendency to always see ourselves in the story. We tend to identify with the central character of films and novels, and we tend to see our own lives as episodic narratives, highlighted by a few dramatic moments.

Some of us have developed classroom role-playing activities based on our experiences. One Marine veteran of Danang, Thom Masterson, uses the Vietnam Veterans Memorial as a focal point. His unassuming manner belies the power of his technique. He asks several students to write on the board the names of their close friends and brothers. You can imagine the rest. For some students, this is their first revelation of the pain of lives lost in war.

Although noncombatant veterans often feel awkward and think their own experiences are too tame to be of worth, we know otherwise. In fact, many of the peacetime or basic training stories resonate deeply with students because they deal with the fundamental human issues with which young people struggle every day: peer pressure, fear of failure, being bullied, challenges to loyalty, and matters of identity and core values.

We have been surprised to discover that while nearly every student treats veteran speakers with respect and interest, sometimes the most responsive listeners are at-risk youngsters, some of whom are or were gang members, many of whom have been perpetrators of or witnesses to violence.

These young people immediately recognize parallels between their own experiences and those of veterans. This has enormously energized many of our speakers and has generated terrific demand for their services in after-school programs, alternative schools, and similar places where young people are desperate for some low key guidance from caring community adults.

These opportunities are available to veterans in every community who want to help young people understand the Vietnam War and to understand themselves. With training and support, veterans can find this to be an effective and fulfilling way to honor the individuals on the Wall by continuing our service to America.

Well, Jimmy, I just found your name [on the online Directory of Names]! I pass the cemetery many times & still I remember your funeral service like it was yesterday. I never told you, as a friend, that I loved you . . . so listen as the Angels speak, "Jimmy, my dear friend, I love you."
                                                                    Linda

The Wall That Heals
By Monica Worth

Monica Worth directs The Wall That Heals, *the national touring exhibition that features a replica of the Vietnam Veterans Memorial. This exhibition includes a mobile museum on the sacrifices of Vietnam veterans, and educational material on the Vietnam War.*

Even sitting behind a folding table inside a tent marked "Information Center," a volunteer can feel the tide of emotion gathering around visitors to The Wall That Heals.

Veterans approach the table, focused intently on the green directories lined up along its length. Each book contains all of the names inscribed on "the Wall." Opening the heavy volumes, an intimate journey begins. For many, this is no easy trip. Some clutch scribbled lists of names. Absorbed in their search, they flip back and forth through the pages finding friend after fallen friend. Others stand before a crowded page and stare at a single string of letters, a name, perhaps last seen embroidered on a buddy's battered uniform. Voices, names, images from the past begin to rise through 30 years of everyday life, of marriage and family, kids and carpools. Soon, each will turn quietly from the table and face the Wall.

Neighbors and friends, remembering their own "Vietnam" experiences, begin another passage. The names they seek may ring in memory from the loudspeaker at a high school football game, or smile from the pages of a yearbook. The clear division of ranks so common then, of pacifist and hawk, of those for a policy of military intervention and those opposed to it, begins to rise in memory. A generation that marched toward the future in two separate columns is about to be reunited at The Wall That Heals.

The last quarter of the 20th century has been marked by extraordinary explorations of history. From King Tut to the raising of the Titanic, images and artifacts now routinely travel around the globe and through time. Each exhibition is fascinating, memorable, enlightening—but rarely transforming. The Wall That Heals has the power to changes lives. Names carved in singular tributes on gravestones and hometown memorials assume their place in history when touched among the 58,214 inscribed on the face of the Wall. Those who search the names for memories find their images reflected side by side, hawk and dove, united in survival and in loss.

The Wall That Heals soon disappears from the local landscape. But it leaves behind a renewed opportunity for recognition and reunion. Similarities begin to outweigh historic differences. Our shared lessons of Vietnam are welcomed home.

On The Road With The Wall
By Linda Anderson

Linda Anderson has been married to John Anderson, a former medic with F Troop, 8th Cavalry in Vietnam, since his return from the war. Before their responsibilities as site managers of The Wall That Heals *kept them too busy, they coordinated the annual* Run For The Wall *motorcycle Memorial Day pilgrimage from California to the Wall.*

During our visit to Port Washington, WI, we had thousands of visitors come by to view The Wall That Heals. One couple came to pay their respects at 11:30 at night. It seems that they had just come from their wedding reception. The bride was still in her gown, the groom in his tux! I didn't hear their story, but obviously it was very important to them to spend an hour at the site before heading off on a honeymoon to start their lives together.

While in Vancouver, WA I met a lady who lost her fiancé in Vietnam 30 years ago and had never married. She felt that having the Wall come to town was a sign to take care of old business and get on with her life. She planned to contact his family, reminisce, and try to let go of the past. She spent a long time in front of her fiancé's name on the Wall. Such love and devotion is truly touching. It never ceases to amaze me how the Wall, and this traveling Wall, has helped people find solace and closure.

While in Port Angeles, WA on Father's Day, I got a whole new perspective on what many consider a day necessitating the purchase of ugly ties. Here, it seemed like people were embracing the true spirit of Father's

Day. There were children and grandchildren, fathers and sons, taking time out of their day's activities to visit the Wall. The notes they left telling Dad about the new grandkids were frequently accompanied by photographs. Walking along the Wall was a four-hanky experience.

Another unusual experience happened in Dolores, CO, when Tony Two Feathers presented us with a 300-year-old feather that his "grandfathers" gave to him upon his return from Vietnam. He told us that he had been looking to "retire" the feather and couldn't think of a better place for it to stay than with his brothers and sisters on the Wall.

These are just a very few of the wonderful experiences my husband John and I have encountered traveling across America. We feel truly honored to be able to share the Wall "magic" in the many towns and cities we have the pleasure of visiting. We hope you will be able to have the chance to visit The Wall That Heals when we come to your town.

Afterword

The Vietnam Veterans Memorial Fund was incorporated in 1979. What was our main mission then? To honor those service members who had served in Vietnam, one of the most controversial wars in the 20th century, by building a memorial. Taking only three years, with help from Americans from all walks of life, we built that memorial, and it is located on the Washington Mall between the Washington Monument and the Lincoln Memorial.

Our main mission today is just as important as it was almost twenty years ago—to preserve the legacy of the Vietnam Veterans Memorial and educate about the impact of the Vietnam War on American culture.

What do we mean by "preserving the legacy?" We're talking about the legacy of healing. Not only the individual healing of family members, veterans, and others whose lives were inexorably changed due to their sacrifices during the war and those lost whose names are on the Wall, but the healing necessitated by the divisiveness of the era. We as a nation needed to heal.

And the Wall is still accomplishing that healing. Many of our programs further that goal as well: **Name Rubbings** are provided at no cost to those who are unable to visit the Wall in Washington, DC; our **In Memory** program honors those service members who died prematurely due to their service and yet whose deaths are not directly combat-related; **Healing Connections**, a search database used to unite veterans with their buddies or their buddies' relatives; annual ceremonies at the Wall on **Memorial Day** and **Veterans Day**, among others.

Our educational component is equally wide ranging. **The Wall That Heals,** our half-scale traveling wall, is accompanied by a museum, which illustrates the sacrifices and accomplishments of Vietnam veterans. This brings the healing home to cities and towns around America, as well as educating today's students who had not even been born when the Wall went up. Much of our energies and resources are going into a nationwide educational initiative that will provide teachers the curriculum and original materials essential to teaching about the Vietnam War. We also provide books—like the one you're holding in your hand right now—to individuals and schools around the country.

These are just a few of our vital projects. The Memorial could never have been built without the generosity of Americans from all walks of life. Without your continued caring and support, none of these vital programs will be possible. Thank you for helping the healing—and learning—continue.

VIETNAM VETERANS MEMORIAL FUND

The Memorial Fund continues to provide important programs. This book is part of our educational program. It will be sent to high schools throughout the United States. The Memorial Fund has other missions as well. Some of our ongoing programs are:

The Young Americans Vietnam War Era Studies Project which involves an extensive curriculum guide for high school teachers and an expansive web site. The comprehensive, multi-disciplinary curriculum gives a historical and sociological review of America's experience during the Vietnam War. We encourage teachers and veterans to work together to expand on the vague story given in textbooks.

Legacy Society which is helping the Memorial Fund to expand the schedule of the Traveling Wall and Museum and to develop our extensive educational programs in America's schools.

The Wall That Heals which brings the healing power of the Wall to hometowns and cities across America. The traveling half-scale replica of the Wall is accompanied by a traveling museum about the Vietnam War, the Wall, and the era.

In Memory which honors veterans of Vietnam who died as a result of the war, but whose names do not appear on the Wall. A special ceremony is held on the third Monday of April each year.

Healing Connections which assists people in their search for others whose loved ones were casualties of the Vietnam War.

Veterans Day and Memorial Day Ceremonies which are held each year at the Wall and The Wall That Heals.

Vietnam Veterans Memorial Fund is a 501(c)(3) nonprofit organization and its funding comes from grants and gifts from the general public.

If you would like more information on our programs or are interested in supporting the Memorial Fund, please contact us at the following address:

VIETNAM VETERANS MEMORIAL FUND
1012 14th Street, NW, Suite 201
Washington, DC 20005-3406
202-393-0090 *phone,* 202-393-0029 *fax*
www.vvmf.org *website,* vvmf@vvmf.org *email*